JACK JOHNSON

Of the series

"They Didn't Know It Couldn't Be Done"

Sal Fradella

Branden Publishing Company

© Copyright 1990
by Salvatore James Fradella

Library of Congress Cataloging-in-Publication Data

Fradella, Sal, 1952-
    Jack Johnson / Sal Fradella.
        p. cm.
    "They didn't know it couldn't be done."
    Includes bibliographical references.
    ISBN 0-8283-1931-6 : $7.95
    1. Johnson, Jack, 1878-1946. 2. Boxers (Sports)--
United States--Biography. I. Title.
GV1132.J7F73   1989
796.8'3'092--dc20
[B]   89-38015
                                 CIP

BRANDEN PUBLISHING COMPANY, Inc.
17 Station Street
PO Box 843 Brokline Village
Boston, MA 02147

DEDICATION

I dedicate this book as I dedicate my life, to my beautiful wife Cheryl, who has made all the difference.

ACKNOWLEDGMENTS

I would like to thank the friends and professionals who helped me in their own special ways to complete a work I am most proud of: Jim Jacobs, Cordelia Campbell Greer, Ron Bronk, Steve Acunto, Wolf Cowen, Pat Amazalorso, Dr. Sophie Welisch, Marge Lopuzzo, Judy Rozanski, Jane Northshield, Fred Hotchkiss, Marion Wyskida, the staffs of the Library of Congress and the Croton Free Public Library and, of course, my old and close friend, Dave Cohen, who introduced me to the magic of Pyscho-Cybernetics in 1971. Special thanks to three students whose criticism helped in the final copy: Jacqueline Bowe, Lorraine McGuire and Karen Flanagan.

Photographs on the following pages are reproduced by permission of:
Library of Congress:
6,7,13,14,15,16,17,18,20,21,25,29,30,34,44,
45,47,52,58,60,61,70,95,100,107
Schomburg Center for Research in Black Culture: 26,27

Grateful acknowledgement is also made for permission to reprint from the following:
Johnson, Jack. *Jack Johnson Is A Dandy: An Autobiography.* New York: Chelsea House Publishers, 1969.

Throughout his life, people said "no" to Jack Johnson. But Johnson believed he had a right to succeed and that no one, not strangers, not even friends had the right to set limits on his ambition.

Jack Johnson did not lead an easy life. But he trusted his own judgement; he believed in his abilities and he was willing to work to achieve the goals he set for himself.

Jack Johnson became Heavyweight Champion of the World and one of the most famous fighters of all time because he knew it doesn't matter how many people say "you can't", so long as you believe you can.

Muhammad Ali

MUHAMMAD ALI

INTRODUCTION

JACK JOHNSON is the first book of my series, "They Didn't Know It *Couldn't* Be Done." Each book will focus on the outstanding life achievement of a different individual. Meant to inspire, "They Didn't Know It *Couldn't* Be Done" is history told as a story, a story with a distinct and living message: SUCCESS. By delving into the triumphs of these people, against the backdrop of the time period in which they lived and the hardships they endured, you will clearly understand why "success is the result of choice, not chance."

Jack Johnson was professional boxing's first black heavyweight champion. The aspect of Johnson's life explored herein, that is, the success story which made him part of this series, is his historic fight in 1910 against James J. Jeffries, a man popularly referred to as the Great White Hope. Be certain, however, that this is far more than the story of a mere prize fight. For you will visit a time period when a black champion - because of his color - was forced to take on those outside of the ring who were determined to sweep him and his blackness from their midst. And yet, despite events that threatened to consume him, Jack Johnson was able to turn adversity into one of the great success stories of this century. In short, it makes for a human drama unequalled in sports history.

But I am getting ahead of myself. Let me take this moment to urge you to read this book and those forthcoming for more than historical content. Read also to uncover the common denominator that ties you to Jack Johnson and the other dynamic people of "They Didn't Know It *Couldn't* Be Done."

And what is that common denominator? In simple terms, it is the power of the human potential - the stuff that all successes are made of. Indeed, if this series can inspire you to use your potential to the fullest, then it will have served its purpose well.

And now let me begin my story about Jack Johnson - the man who defied the odds because he "didn't know it *couldn't* be done."

PART ONE
Jack Johnson: The Man and the Times That Shaped Him

He was one of the most hated men of his time, yet could have been loved. His golden smile could warm hearts, but chilled them more often than not. He sought respect, yet was showered with contempt; and though he had stolen nothing, he was despised for stealing a symbolic treasure.

His name was Jack Johnson. On December 26, 1908, he did the unthinkable in Sydney, Australia - he fought for the heavyweight title of the world. When his hand was raised in victory, the unthinkable became the unforgivable - for Jack Johnson was black.

Because of racial hatred and misunderstanding, his blackness changed this from a sporting to a social event, an event that shook society to its racist foundation. For when it was over, white supremacists knew that they, the masters, had been mastered.

But white supremacists rejected this outcome. To them, the heavyweight crown was the symbol of American manhood. That this symbol should now pass to a member of a so-called inferior breed was considered an outrage.

But to rid themselves of this outrage, white supremacists would first have to be rid of Jack Johnson.

An unlikely hero, John Arthur Johnson was born March 31, 1878 in the seaport city of Galveston, Texas. Although both parents stressed education, he quit school after the fifth grade and immediately went to work. While still a youngster, Johnson painted milk wagons, exercised race horses, baked bread and unloaded ships on the Galveston docks.

He eventually became a janitor in a local gym. It was here that Lil' Arthur - Johnson's nickname for beating up a neighborhood bully - discovered the sport that would make him a champion and legend.

Each day on the job, he took note of everything around him - the sounds and smells of the gym, the sweat of hard work, the sight of achievement through discipline. His senses came alive.

Inspired, young Johnson began training with the gym's weights and pulleys. But he did more than develop his body. He now dedicated himself to the science of boxing.

In what became a routine, Johnson sparred, shadow-boxed, hit the heavy bag, the speed bag, jumped rope, studied the technique of other fighters and practiced the defensive skills that would become his trademark.

He also bought two pair of boxing gloves. With these in hand, Lil' Arthur searched the black neighborhoods for opponents, so that when he found one, he would challenge him to a bout, toss him a pair of gloves and delight onlookers with his skill. After years of such drifting and brawling, Jack Johnson was hailed as the best black boxer in Galveston, Texas.

But in spite of this success, young Johnson grew impatient with his hometown. He now dreamed of worlds beyond its borders - of fame and wealth and opportunity.

The unknown did not frighten him. It made him dream bigger. And when those dreams became big enough, our hero packed and left home.

Drifting at first through Chicago, New York and Boston, Lil' Arthur was a teenager bound by no set plan.

He trained in different gyms and worked whenever possible as a sparring partner. When the money from sparring could not supply him with his daily bread, he worked as a laborer.

It was a hard life. But this was the price he was willing to pay, the price for success.

Hunger, loneliness, poverty, disappointment - these were mere details of the battle, hardships that he knew he would overcome through perseverance. In time, the experience proved valuable. It toughened him and shattered any doubt about his true purpose. He was a fighter!

Despite his youth, this was no boyish pastime or foggy dream of future greatness. It was his way of life - his life's blood.

And, as the first weeks and months away from home turned into a year, young Johnson's hunger to succeed brought him a wider range of opportunity.

In different gyms, he was invited to spar with better fighters. He even fought circus boxers who challenged their audiences for money. When informal bouts were held on docks or in strange alleyways, Lil' Arthur was always first on line to do battle.

Although slender, he had grown muscular and tough, and his ever sharpening boxing skills made him a winner in every contest.

Certain that the worst was now behind him and that the heavyweight crown lay ahead, John Arthur Johnson, in 1897, took the next big step into his dream - he became a professional boxer. The sport would never be the same.

From the moment he turned pro until the day he became champ in 1908, Johnson would box an astounding 77 times. This was more than most heavyweights would dare fight in a career. Of these, he lost three. But he learned from his mistakes.

And with experience, talent and raw power, he became the most deadly fighter of his day, and, perhaps, the greatest heavyweight champion of all time.

But before achieving this goal there would be a lesson to learn about the world of which he would be champion. For that world was going to reject him as well as the idea of a black man wearing the heavyweight crown.

If herein lies Jack Johnson's dilemma, so too emerges his greatness.

More than anything else, in Jack Johnson's world blacks were considered a "white man's burden," slow, dull, inferior. In keeping with that status, they were segregated from whites like the carriers of a plague.

Not even the United States Supreme Court would undo this injustice. With the *Plessy vs. Ferguson* decision of 1896, "separate but equal" became the legal catch-phrase that millions of white supremacists had been waiting to hear.

Now, with the Constitution firmly behind them, they could separate further from the race they despised.

In time, other Jim Crow laws, all designed to maintain a social wall between white and black, were allowed to seep even deeper into the American landscape. Dating back, in many cases, to the end of Reconstruction and now upheld in *Plessy vs Ferguson*, the policies of Jim Crow proved difficult for blacks to overcome.

Indeed, there were many places that would not even have blacks without restricting them to the "Colored Section."

Churches, hotels, schools, restrooms and even prisons served as daily reminders that as America advanced into the Twentieth Century, blacks would remain on that fine line between slavery and freedom. It was a place which white supremacists would not let them forget.

John L. Sullivan

Heavyweight championship boxing was no different. In 1892, champ John L. Sullivan challenged all contenders, "first come - first served." But there was one condition. "I will not fight a Negro," he declared. "I never have and never will." True to his word, John L. never did.

And so the heavyweight crown, like the Presidency of the United States, was off limits to blacks - another betrayal of the American Dream.

Boxing's color line, however, was not the result of one man. It was established because whites, many whites, feared the possible result of an interracial bout.

While whites believed that their champion would beat a black contender, they still worried that something could go wrong - perhaps a lucky punch. And should a black man win the title, other blacks might then become uppity and difficult to control.

They too might demand their chance to achieve the American Dream, to become doctors, or senators, or to move into better neighborhoods - white neighborhoods. They might even conclude that they were not the white man's burden after all, but rather, his equal.

On that basis, "We Cater to White Trade Only," became law in heavyweight championship bouts. Even to consider breaking it was an outrage. The white race had too much to lose and nothing to gain.

Jack Johnson would destroy such ideas. White man's burden! En route to the title, he was more like the white man's nightmare.

With cat-like precision and skill, Johnson overwhelmed opponents. By doing this, he made a mockery of any theories about black inferiority. So much so that it became easier for white racists to hate Jack Johnson than to explain him, a fact made all too clear by their countless plots to dethrone and destroy him after he won the heavyweight crown.

And yet, this hatred did not stem simply from his being the first black champion. What worsened matters was Johnson's character and antics outside the ring.

Despite clearly defined social barriers, Jack Johnson enjoyed the lifestyle of which most white men could only dream. Proud and unyielding, he refused to bend to the whims of others. Nor would he be told how he, as a black man, should live within society.

Instead, he made his own rules. He lived by his own standards. As soon as the money and prestige of success rolled in, he also became the exception to any rule he chose.

At a time when blacks were avoided by lowly local politicians, Jack Johnson conversed with European royalty.

At a time when whites stereotyped black males in a pair of overalls, Jack Johnson hired a maid just to care for his wardrobe.

At a time when many blacks were buried beneath poverty and debt, Jack Johnson sipped wine through a straw, owned an integrated nightclub, drove expensive sports cars and proudly mounted a diamond onto one of his gold studded teeth.

At a time when black men were lynched for simply looking at white women, Jack Johnson looked at, caroused with, and married white women.

And at a time when racist theory taught that the black man was not genetically a man, Jack Johnson proved that he was not only a man - but his own man.

Needless to say, the social implications were clear. By refusing to stay on the "black side" of the color line, Johnson had become a symbol of rebellion; worse, he threatened order, the status quo.

But when the white establishment tried to make him yield to its authority, he grew more defiant.

He was once arrested for abducting a white woman. However groundless the charge, it was still expected that he show fear, submission. But this was a gross miscalculation.

Upon entering his jail cell, Johnson showed anything but fear when he demanded that the guards supply him with candles, cigars and a case of champagne.

On the day of his arraignment, our hero was even worse. He strolled into court half an hour late with a cigar in his mouth and a bright, arrogant smile on his face, laughing at those who would destroy him.

"I have the right to choose who my mate shall be without the dictation of any man," Johnson told the press, insisting that he was not a slave. "I have eyes and a heart and when they fail to tell me who I shall have for mine, I want to be put away in a lunatic asylum."

Indeed, if Lil' Arthur was defiant, then defiance was a badge he wore with honor.

These public shenanigans, though, were not separate from his boxing career. One was usually a reaction to the other.

Since turning pro, John Arthur Johnson had confronted racism so deeply rooted that lesser individuals would have shrunk before it, believing themselves victims of a racist plot. But Jack Johnson would not shrink. Nor could he.

Each time the ring reminded him of his second class citizenship, he grew more determined, more focused, more angry. And he remembered.

He remembered the Battle Royal, the brutal contest where eight or more black men fought in the ring at the same time. Often naked, blindfolded and wearing Sambo masks, they would swing wildly at each other until one man was left standing. His reward: loose change thrown from the crowd. Although dating back to his early career, the Battle Royal was a stinging humiliation Jack Johnson would never forgive.

He remembered that as his commitment to boxing increased, so did his fears and suspicions. Traveling to fights as a stowaway aboard freight trains - in trips that took him from coast to coast - he was often hunted, clubbed by police, arrested, imprisoned and called every foul racial slur his ears could stand.

He remembered that when he reached championship caliber, he was treated instead like a third rate pug. Despite his victorious record, he was forced to chase the reigning heavyweight champion, Tommy Burns, across the world for two years.

The purpose of this hunt was to pressure Burns into giving Lil' Arthur what was rightfully his - a chance to fight for the heavyweight crown.

He remembered that to lure Burns into signing the contract, he had to agree to two conditions that would have been unthinkable had he been white.

First, Burns would receive $35,000 of the overall purse. This left Lil' Arthur with barely enough money to pay expenses.

Second, Burns insisted that Mr. Hugh McIntosh referee the bout. An admitted close friend of the champion, it was widely believed that McIntosh was his manager as well.

Tommy Burns

And Johnson remembered that when the contract was finally signed, Tommy Burns publicly referred to him as nigger, coon and coward - hateful words that grew worse as the fight approached.

Nevertheless, it was now time, payback time - for Tommy Burns, for Jim Crow, for every vestige of white supremacy. And on that historic twenty-sixth of December, 1908, Jack Johnson did pay back. He paid in full.

With the world's attention focused in on Sydney, Australia, he erupted viciously upon the squat body of Tommy Burns. So shocking was the sight of a black challenger demolishing a white champion, that police stopped the filming of the bout in round fourteen, moments before Burns hit the canvas.

Johnson could easily have ended the bout earlier. He chose instead to prolong the beating, saying: "I figured that Burns had something coming to him. I certainly wished to give him his $35,000 worth." It was a task he performed with pleasure.

But for Jack Johnson triumph and trouble were usually one and the same. It seemed that no sooner was one battle fought and won than another peeked over the horizon to take its place. Could this time be any different?

Even before leaving the ring as the newly crowned champion, Lil' Arthur had already been targeted for a counter-attack.

White supremacists everywhere were suddenly united in a common cause against him. Equal to vengeance was their demand for redemption. And they were determined to have both.

Thus, it was time for a hero, a Great White Hope, to rise up and restore to white America the two things taken by Jack Johnson: the heavyweight crown and the sacred honor of the Caucasian race.

To have one without the other was impossible. The two were now inseparable.

PART TWO
Enter James J. Jeffries, the Great White Hope

The Great White Hope

The unanimous choice for a white hope was James J. Jeffries, the retired heavyweight champ. All who hated Jack Johnson and the thought of a black champion in a white man's world, could take comfort in Jeffries.

He was a skyscraper of a man, massive in both size and strength, who in his glory weighed 220 pounds and towered at 6 feet, 2 inches.

Ironically, he was quite agile in spite of his bulk. He could run 100 yards in just 11 seconds and high jump almost 6 feet.

In the heat of battle, it was Jeffries' style always to move forward, to bring the fight to his opponent, so that he looked like an on-coming locomotive that could not be stopped.

And with hands that seemed to contain dynamite, Jeffries could knock an opponent into the world of dreams and peacefulness, a practice he repeated in more than three-quarters of his fights.

During his reign, Big Jim thoroughly dominated the heavyweight division, beating almost every top contender twice. Before running out of worthy opposition in 1904, he could boast not only of an undefeated record but that he had never been knocked off his feet.

When the time came to retire, Jeffries, with the bearing of a king, handpicked two contenders to fight for his crown. He then refereed the elimination bout between them in 1905.

The two men who fought, Marvin Hart and Jack Root, were universally recognized as second raters, both of whom Big Jim could beat on the same night.

When Marvin Hart won, he was thus dubbed a pretender to the throne. The invincibility myth of James J. Jeffries had begun.

Be that as it may, with all ring business behind him, Big Jim turned to the comfort of his California farm and announced that he would "never fight again," a promise he fully intended to keep. When he ballooned over the next few years to 320 pounds, it seemed the pledge would not be broken.

Destiny, however, can entangle a person into its own web. With the crowning of a black champion, especially one like Jack Johnson, it was clear that events would soon destroy Big Jim's desire for comfort and seclusion.

The first voice calling Jeffries out of exile was that of author Jack London, who reported the Johnson-Burns fight for the *New York Herald*.

After describing it as a fight between a "playful Ethiopian and a small and futile white man," London made an emotional appeal to Jeffries. He was speaking for everyone who compared Jack Johnson's victory with Armaggedon: "But one thing remains, Jeffries must emerge from his alfalfa farm and wipe that golden smile off Jack Johnson's face. Jeff, it's up to you!"

Although moved emotionally, Jeffries could not be budged. He was enjoying the charms of rustic life. His overblown physique was proof.

To give up such leisure for the hardships of the gym was simply out of the question. He was retired and that was that.

If the white race wanted a "white hope" to save them, then they would have to get somebody else. He was not interested. The issue was closed.

Jack London

Jack Johnson would change all that. Within one year of making chopped meat of Tommy Burns, the black champion easily defeated five more white hopes.

Frustrated by Johnson's success and eager to reassert the superiority of their race, white supremacists turned to Jeffries with unprecedented emotion.

Already a looming figure in retirement, Jim Jeffries the man was suddenly dwarfed by Jim Jeffries the myth.

Those seeking relief in him easily believed that he once cured himself of pneumonia by drinking a case of whiskey in two days. To prove that Jeffries had the qualities of a god, a story circulated that a doctor had once diagnosed him as being "not human."

And what made all of this so sweet was the widely held belief that Big Jim felt nothing but hatred for the black champion.

Believing Johnson to be an endangered species, white supremacists across America assured themselves that one day Jim Jeffries would "kill that damn nigger once and for all."

Amidst the storytelling and myth-making, added pressure was put upon Jeffries by a daily avalanche of mail. He was assured that he could not only annihilate Johnson, but that it was his duty to do so. "Jeff, it's up to you!"

Whenever seen in public, people were drawn to him like scavengers upon a dead carcass. It seemed as though everyone wanted to get close to the man who would kill Jack Johnson.

Flattered by the confidence and affection showered upon him, Jeffries was still doubtful about returning to the ring. After all, he was now thirty-five years old, grossly out of shape, and his extra poundage made him look more like a beached whale than a god.

If blood was indeed thicker than water, he also had to contend with his father's public vow to disown him should he so much as step into the same ring with Jack Johnson.

All in all, there was still something enticing about the emotion heaped upon him.

In time it took on a hypnotic quality, as the dual theme of his invincibility and the honor of his race were drummed continuously into his ears.

Slowly but surely the pressure took its toll until, finally, after being told so many times that he was a god in human form, Jim Jeffries believed in his own myth. Retirement was over.

On December 1, 1909, he signed the contract to fight Jack Johnson.

Immediately dubbed the "Fight of the Century," the bout was scheduled for July 4, 1910, in San Francisco.

For Jim Jeffries it was a call to arms, a chance to wipe away forever the "golden smile" that had brought such misery to his race. "I realize full well just what depends upon me," he later assured white America, "and I am not going to disappoint the public."

Good would at last triumph over evil, or so Big Jim hoped. But now started the process - the gargantuan process - of whipping his enormous body into shape, a task that would put the invincibility myth to the test.

"It amuses me to hear this talk of Jeffries claiming the championship," Johnson laughed. "Why, when a Mayor leaves his office he's an ex-Mayor, isn't he? When a champion leaves the ring he's an ex-champion. Well, that is Jeffries; if he wants to try to get the championship back then I'm willing to take him on."

Beneath this casual response, Jack Johnson was ecstatic. The fight was his dream come true.

On the one hand, the money offered was a pot of gold. Tex Rickard, the promoter and proprietor of the bout, guaranteed both men $101,000 and two-thirds of the movie rights. The split would be 60-40 with the winner taking the larger percentage.

Extra icing was added to this luscious cake with a promised cash bonus of $10,000 for each man upon signing the contract.

Johnson stood to make more than $350,000, a sum that would assure his splendid lifestyle for at least the foreseeable future.

More importantly, of course, this was the chance to prove that he indeed was the undisputed champion. Many people believed, or at least tried to convince themselves, that Jeffries still reigned supreme because he did not lose the title in the heat of battle.

Instead, he had passed it on to Marvin Hart, who then lost it to Tommy Burns. Because Hart and Burns could not be considered true champions, as neither had beaten Big Jim in the ring, Johnson too had to be a pretender to the throne, a phony that the real champion would soon conquer.

Harassed and criticized for being a fake, a paper champion, Johnson was thrilled at this opportunity to settle the matter once and for all.

"Coming out of Retirement"

PART THREE
The Days Before the Fight

The Fight of the Century immediately faced problems. Although it enjoyed the support of California Governor James J. Gillette, the bout seemed doomed before it started.

Reformers throughout America, determined, sanctimonious and organized, were bent on stopping it. Prizefighting, like liquor and other forms of vice, was taboo to them, something out of place in an enlightened age. It had to be eradicated!

One million postcards from Cincinnati were addressed to Governor Gillette with a common statement: "Stop The Fight. This Is The 20th Century."

Pressure also came in flesh and blood. Fifty ministers, hoping that their presence would shame the governor into changing his mind, had assembled on the steps of the state capital to pray.

From pulpit to editorial page anger against the bout was strong and spontaneous; and feelings were hardly soothed with rumors of a fixed fight.

Indeed, word had circulated that Jeffries could not get into shape and that for an enormous sum Lil' Arthur had agreed to take a dive.

Although false, the rumor was taken seriously. And it helped to convince a doubting public that boxing was just one step above feeding Christians to the lions.

Governor Gillette, a true politician, immediately sensed the damage such a scandal could have for him. With political ambitions to go to Washington, he started to waver in his commitment to the fight.

In the end, however, it was economics and not morality that kayoed the fight in San Francisco.

Word reached Gillette, by way of Congressman William S. Bennett of the House Committee on Foreign Relations, that should the fight take place as scheduled, it could end plans for San Francisco's hosting of the Panama-Pacific Exposition of 1915. This made the governor's decision easy.

In terms of dollars and cents the fight would be a financial bonanza for only one week. The exposition, on the other hand, would sprout good fortune for San Francisco for an entire summer.

Consequently, with less than three weeks left until fight time, Governor Gillette announced that the Fight of the Century would have to leave town.

Not one to be held down for long, Tex Rickard made an agreement with Governor Denver Dickerson of Nevada for the fight to be held in Reno. Once assured that the bout would be legitimate, the governor gave his blessing.

The world now turned its attention to Reno.

Tex Rickard

Nevada at the turn of the century was like an island unto itself. While the reform movement brought endless change to other parts of the country, this Western state seemed isolated from its constant barrage, content to let puritan morality sweep past it.

Vice was not viewed here as sinful. It was seen instead as harmless entertainment, a pastime to be enjoyed.

Many fortunes had been lost and won in this desert community, and with the lure of forbidden fruit, her borders were invaded once more by those seeking the benefits of the upcoming fight. All were hoping that new fortunes could now be made.

The clientele that arrived, though, did nothing to improve Nevada's image, a state most outsiders already considered the Devil's work.

Thieves, thugs, gamblers, drunks, pick-pockets, hoboes, hired assassins and almost every other type of "moral degenerate," descended in mass upon Reno. According to the more than 500 reporters present, the desert town, in the weeks just prior to the fight, had become a virtual "who's who" in the world of crime.

On hand was the noted bank robber Cincinnati Slim, as was Won Let, the hatchet man for the New York branch of the Hip Sing Tong, who was rumored to have killed between twenty and thirty of his fellow Chinese.

Also expected to arrive by the opening bell was the Sundance Kid, the notorious bad man later to become part of America's folklore.

It seemed as if nobody was safe from those lurking in and out of the shadows. Even Jack Johnson felt it necessary to carry a gun. As an added precaution, he announced that his friend and bodyguard, Cal McVey, would patrol with a shotgun should there be any signs of trouble.

Although careful, Jack Johnson was having the time of his life. Everything was falling into place.

During training sessions he worked hard, yet paced himself skillfully. He was in charge of his workouts at all times, insisting that his seconds follow his directions to the letter.

As the fight drew nearer, Johnson's already magnificent body blossomed into a finely tuned machine. Every part functioned as it should - with precision and at full capacity. He was nothing short of magnificent.

"I have never seen a man who can whip Jack Johnson as he stands today," the Nevada Governor told reporters after observing the champion work out, " and I am forced to bet on him."

Such words just added to the good will and confidence of the Johnson training camp.

When not preparing for the fight, Johnson relaxed and enjoyed himself. He frequently participated in poker and baseball games, entertained friends with his bass fiddle and clowned freely with members of the press. Everything about the champion showed confidence.

Yet, to many on the outside, this tranquil, laid back attitude was interpreted as a sure sign of an inferior race.

Critics of Jack Johnson, who once again relied upon racist theory, believed him unable to understand the danger he was in. In their view, the true black was happy go lucky, stupid and incapable of looking into the future.

They felt that if Johnson could look ahead to the upcoming fight that he would be quaking with fear rather than playing games or his bass fiddle.

With this in mind, they therefore dismissed Lil' Arthur's courage and confidence as a sham: proof of a doomed race, proof of a doomed champion.

But our hero knew himself better than that. Supremely confident in his ability, he could even wish the best for his opponent.

In gracious, dignified tones he said to the public, "Every fighter on the eve of his fight declares that he hopes the best man wins. I am quite sincere when I say that I do, and if Mr. Jeffries knocks me out or gains a decision over me, I will go into his corner and congratulate him as soon as I am able.

"My congratulations will not be fake. I mean it. Should I meet defeat I will have no excuse to offer and will proclaim Mr. Jeffries king of them all."

While Johnson appeared positive, the mood in the Jeffries' camp was quite different. From the beginning it seemed as if a dark foreboding cloud was hovering above with a game plan of its own, determined to keep matters in a constant state of gloom.

For those in his inner circle, one thing was certain - he was not the Jim Jeffries of old.

Gone was the tremendous strength that served him so well in days past, for it had been drained in shedding almost one hundred pounds of fat. His judgement of timing and distance, those two indispensable tools in whose absence a champion could be reduced to a mere hack, were both noticeably and dangerously off; and his mighty "left," the one-time scourge of the heavyweight division, seemed unable to resurrect itself from the pages of history.

Emotionally overwrought, Jeffries was either restless or irritable. In a word, he was a "grouch." This ill-humored mood was given a further jolt when he learned that John L. Sullivan, who was in town to report the bout for the *New York Times,* had publicly remarked that the fight looked like a "frame-up."

By the eve of the bout, Jeffries was coming unwound. He lost his appetite and in spite of retiring early to bed, spent most of the night pacing about like a man deeply troubled.

Ironically, for Jim Jeffries the "white man" had become his burden; so many loved him; so many believed in him; so many depended on him; so many wanted to make Big Jim the means to their end that by fight day the awesome responsibility had taken its toll. Fact was overcoming fiction.

Nevertheless, on July 4, 1910, James Jackson Jeffries arrived at the arena with the hope, if not quite the belief, that he still indeed was invincible. At that moment nothing else would do.

PART FOUR
The Fight of the Century

The first man to enter the ring was Jack Johnson. As he paced about, wrapped snugly in a gray silk robe, he could not help but feel the intense mood in the arena.

Nearly twenty thousand spectators, all stewing in anticipation, had come to bear witness to history. This was the day of reckoning, the day all would be made right.

The excitement was incredible. Everyone seemed consumed by it. Loud, strong voices filled the desert air like a wall of rolling sound.

Above the screams, Lil' Arthur could still hear a volley of racial slurs, all of which were meant for him.

"There were few men of my own race among the spectators," he recalled. "I realized that my victory in this event meant more than on any previous occasion.

"It wasn't just the championship that was at stake - it was my own honor, and in a degree the honor of my race.

"I was well aware of all these things, and I sensed that most of that great audience was hostile to me."

And indeed they were. Moments before he left his dressing room, a brass band played a rousing rendition of "All Coons Look Alike to Me," a song most of the crowd sang along to in an effort to rattle the champ.

But if all this was meant to have a negative effect upon him, it did not work. Jack Johnson showed no sign of fear or anger.

He simply returned their racism with a shake of his cleanly shaven head, a clapping together of his hands and a gleaming profile of the one weapon guaranteed to enrage them - his golden smile.

Matters continued in this way until the deafening noise was suddenly increased twenty-fold. Jim Jeffries was now approaching the ring. Pandemonium broke loose.

It was as though a local hero was returning home after single-handedly winning a war. As he entered the ring with an entourage that included "Gentlemen" Jim Corbett, a former champion and boxing immortal, the excitement grew stronger.

Jeffries looked intimidating. Throwing out his massive chest, he chewed gum and stared menacingly at Johnson.

Rather than return the look, Lil' Arthur turned his back. This was interpreted by the sea of white faces as a sure sign of fear, evidence of what Jim Corbett called Jack Johnson's "yellow streak."

"He daresn't look at him," the audience hooted. "O-oo! Don't let him see him! Don't let him see him!"

One can only imagine what was going through Jim Jeffries' mind at this moment. Betting odds favored him by 10 to 6, while in the hearts of the true believers, he was a 1,000 to 1 shoe-in. John L. Sullivan, James J. Corbett, Robert Fitzsimmons, Tommy Burns and a host of other boxing greats all favored Big Jim.

But was he up to it? Could he shake off the sluggishness that had plagued his workouts? Was he invincible? These and other questions would soon be answered. Destiny could wait no longer.

At the conclusion of the preliminary activities Tex Rickard, who was chosen to referee the bout, signaled for the opening bell. Unlike other championship fights, the two combatants did not shake hands before starting. According to a prearranged agreement, it was decided to suspend this ring tradition, a sure sign that more was at stake than a mere heavyweight title. But by now it did not seem to matter. The Fight of the Century was under way.

With the loud screams still resounding in their ears, James J. Jeffries, as in days past, brought the fight to his opponent.

While he advanced, Johnson showed caution, keeping the on-coming beast at arm's length. His style proved economical. While Jeffries crouched, lunged and swung wildly, the champion countered with straight, perfectly timed rights and lefts.

Ironically, in the clinches, it was Johnson who tossed his opponent with ease, proof that he was the stronger of the two men.

Yet, when the round ended, Jeffries received a loud, reassuring cheer from the crowd. Most of them were still confident that their money had been wisely invested in the big white man.

Round two was basically a repeat performance, with the Jeffries left proving ineffective against Johnson's masterful defense.

In the next round, however, Lil' Arthur connected with a left that was solid enough to noticeably shake up Jeffries. To add insult to injury, he taunted the white hope during clinches. "Come on now, Mr. Jeff," the champion mocked. "Let me see what you got. Do something, man!"

Jeffries, whose face was repeatedly being hit, tried to oblige his tormentor but was being thoroughly outclassed. At the end of round three, the audience, more puzzled than alarmed, kept their hopes high.

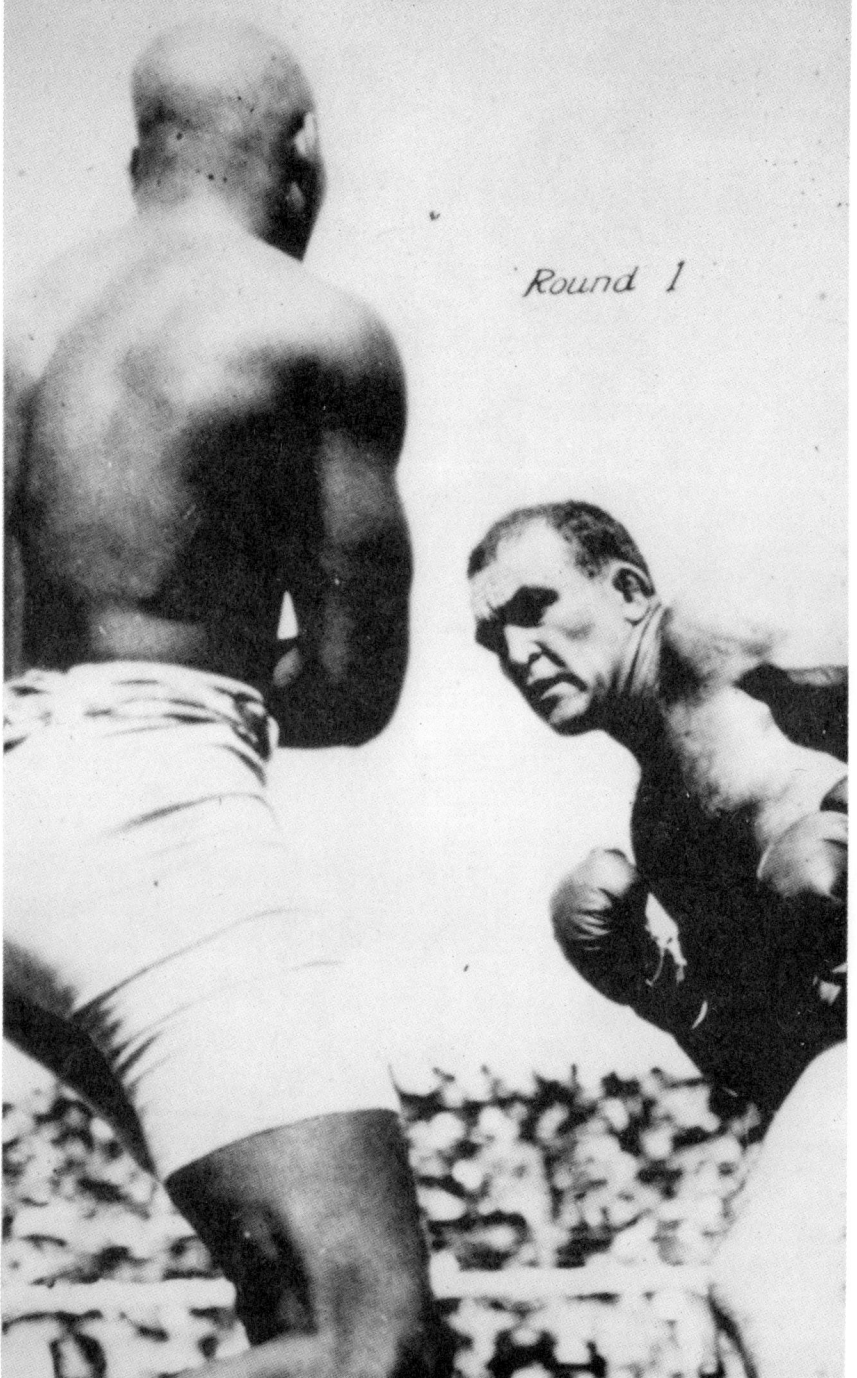
Round 1

By the start of the fourth round Johnson sensed that Jeffries could be had. He immediately went on the offensive, sticking his left into Big Jim's face at will. "I can go on like this all afternoon, Mr. Jeff," he said, as he stepped up the pace. During this round, however, the challenger's supporters took heart; a Jeffries left finally penetrated the champion's defense and cut his lip. "First blood for Jeffries!" the crowd yelled.

But like the Great White Hope himself, this hope too was a sham. What they did not know was that Johnson's lip had been cut while in training. Their man had merely reopened an old wound, a wound for which he would pay dearly with his own blood.

In between rounds, Jeffries barely spoke. He found the tension unbearable; worse, as the fight progressed, his confidence eroded.

What was to be done? It was too late to reconsider. To run and hide was out of the question; and besides, even if he could, his tormentor would soon find him and continue the onslaught.

All that was left was to absorb more punishment and hope for a miracle. Perhaps the black man would tire out or make a mistake.

With the opening of the seventh round, it became clear that there would be no such miracle. Johnson came out quickly and landed a crushing right cross to Jeffries' jaw. From here things only got worse for the white hope.

During the next two rounds he was hit hard and often; it was as if open season had been declared on his face and body.

When he tried to launch a counterattack, Jeffries was further frustrated by the champion's footwork, an asset effectively used by Johnson to keep him out of danger's way.

Clearly showing the signs of battle, Big Jim returned to his corner at the end of round nine, his face marked and swollen, his right eye almost closed and his tired, crumbling torso in desperate need of rest and oxygen.

Amidst these troubles, Jim Corbett battled the champion in his own way.

An admitted and vocal racist, "Gentleman" Jim believed that all black fighters became useless physically when upset emotionally. This prompted him to make faces at the champion and to jeer him with insults, thus bringing the sport to a demeaning low.

Bothered not one iota, Lil' Arthur responded with characteristic arrogance - he manhandled Jeffries and dragged him halfway across the ring to "Gentleman" Jim. "Thought you'd have me fighting wild, didn't you?" the champion mockingly asked. "Who's wild now?" This infuriated Corbett to the point of frenzy, making him anything but a "gentleman."

However, like Jeffries, he too saw the writing clearly on the wall. Rather than endure that golden smile for so worthless a plan, Corbett admitted defeat and stopped his childish antics.

By the end of round twelve it was clear to even the most hard core supporters that as a white hope, James J. Jeffries was about to slip into the past tense. At this point, they were as deflated as he was beaten.

The one-time battle cry of "Jeff, it's up to you!" was fading into memory. It seemed hard to believe that the bloody, disfigured pulp, heaving for air, could now redeem the Caucasian race.

To add to their horror, Jack Johnson was not only proving himself the master, but he was laughing out loud, delighting in his destruction of white hopes and white supremacy.

For Jeffries, round fourteen, like the one before it, was similar to walking into a maze and facing a meat cleaver at every turn. Stinging lefts and rights, their impact tearing at exposed, quivering nerves, cut him to pieces.

Unable to figure out the puzzle and still hoping for a miracle, Jeffries swung wildly. But by now his weary, heavy arms had neither the snap to throw a decisive punch or the strength to block a blow from Johnson.

"How do you feel, Jim?" How do you like it?" Johnson asked as he prolonged the inevitable.

The groggy former champion's nose was now broken and what was left of his face was covered with blood. He could do nothing but absorb whatever punishment Lil' Arthur chose to dish out.

"Does it hurt, Jim?" inquired Johnson as he dismembered Jeffries further. The bell finally ended round fourteen.

Back in his corner Jim Jeffries looked every bit the loser, desolate, quiet, confused. For the past fourteen rounds, he had been made to pay for every slight, every humiliation ever imposed upon Jack Johnson by white supremacists.

Like Tommy Burns, he was learning the hard way that the black champion could be a vicious and vengeful man. Events were now literally beyond his control. Jeffries seemed a doomed man resigned to his fate.

Even Jim Corbett's frantic, emotion-charged lectures about white supremacy and the honor of one's race were unable to rouse him; such words fell only on deaf ears.

At this point Big Jim wanted nothing to do with his race, or, for that matter, its sacred honor.

After all, was it not his race that got him into this mess? And now that he was in it, where were they? What could the white race do to save him now?

Ironically, a legend persists to this day, that an up and coming Jack Johnson once asked to fight Big Jim, the then reigning heavyweight champion of the world. But Jeffries would have none of it, insisting that the bout would not even "draw flies."

What he meant to say, was that as champion he wished to segregate himself from black contenders. He would not cross the color line. In his view, the heavyweight crown was a jewel that should be reserved only for whites. Blacks were not fit to wear it. Yet, for this "championship" fight Big Jim had willingly crossed that color line; and if he still believed blacks unworthy of the title, he would now pay for his arrogance. For the fifteenth round was upon him.

At the sound of the bell, Jeffries came out fighting by simple instinct - he moved toward Johnson. Barely able to see beyond his bloody and slashed eyelids, he walked hopelessly into a nightmare.

Waiting for him, the champion unleased a series of right-left combinations that forced Jeffries to the ropes.

Once there, Johnson connected with a right uppercut and four explosive lefts to the challenger's head.

For the first time in his career Jim Jeffries fell to the canvas; the legend fell with him.

As he lifted his wallowing carcass, the crowd began pleading for an end to the massacre. "Stop it, stop it," they screamed. "Don't let him be knocked out!"

This was certainly a far cry from "Jeff, it's up to you!"

Standing but helpless, Jeffries was chopped down again by a left to the head. This time, however, he suffered the indignity of falling through the ropes.

Exhausted, he seemed content to stay down. But that was more than some ringsiders could bear, as a group of them stepped onto the ring apron and helped Big Jim to his feet.

For all the good it did, he was standing at the count of nine. But the end was now at hand.

It would be merciful to think that Jim Jeffries did not see what happened next. It would have been too frightening.

The look on the champion's face, which for the entire fight had radiated with his gold, glistening smile, suddenly transformed into a vicious glare. Had Jeffries seen this he most likely would have run for cover - but too late.

Johnson moved in quickly and unleashed three consecutive blows, each snapping Jeffries' head back, each powerful and perfectly timed. Their impact sent the Great White Hope crashing back down to the canvas.

This time his cornermen would throw in the towel before Tex Rickard could count to ten.

PART FIVE
Epilogue

The Fight of the Century was over. Though race riots would later break out because of it, the immediate response was quiet.

Those people leaving the arena, most of whom were arrogant a short time before, were now in a sullen mood; they shared in Big Jim's disgrace.

In newspaper offices all across the land white supremacists, recently huddled in hope of good news from Reno, now had to deal with their emotions. They too were silent.

As the baffled and disappointed fans walked off in their own directions, it would not be difficult to imagine that a shrug of the shoulder or a shake of the head in disbelief was all that most of them could now muster.

Yet, whether by news wire or ringside seat they had witnessed together a tremendous athlete, a master of his craft, who put on a pugilistic display as flawless as it was decisive. On that matter there could be no argument.

Jim Jeffries also admitted this fact on board a train that night to California. He was headed back to his "alfalfa farm", the sanctuary he should never have left in the first place.

With his face still resembling an ugly, swollen Halloween mask, and his mood as crestfallen as the crowd he left behind in the arena, the now defunct white hope spoke frankly to reporters. "I could never have whipped Jack Johnson at my best," he said. "I couldn't have hit him. No, I couldn't have reached him in a thousand years."

He was correct - absolutely correct - and this time his retirement from the ring would be permanent.

As for Jack Johnson, he was about to face new troubles. The years ahead would be as burdensome for him as his victory over Jim Jeffries was total; but that is another story in itself.

Let it suffice to say, that Lil' Arthur was defiant until the very end; and that whenever possible he slapped the snoot of the enemy sworn to destroy him - white supremacy.

For the time being, though, he was at the height of his ring career. This was surely a moment of jubilee! After all, he had destroyed the greatest of the great white hopes. Now, he could spoon feed the crow that many of the experts would have to eat.

Despite their predictions, it was he who had been in total control from the opening bell; he who had proved his moral, intellectual and physical superiority; and, like it or not, it was he, Jack Johnson - a black man - who was now the undisputed heavyweight champion of the world. It was a title he seemed destined to hold onto for as long as he chose.

"None can deny," Lil' Arthur said, reflecting on his victory over the Great White Hope, "that I had fought persistently and conscientiously. I had won all I had attained by sheer hard training, fighting and confidence in myself."

Having thus prepared himself to succeed, he was then able to toy with his opponent. And for a short time at least, his demolition of the white hope gave others of his race, many of whom were praying in church for him during the fight, a break from their shackled world.

Jack and Tiny Johnson, his mother

Not since the Emancipation Proclamation were blacks given more reason for rejoicing. It was a triumph they could all enjoy together.

In cities throughout the land, when word spread of Lil' Arthur's victory, thousands upon thousands of blacks, their heads held high and their spirits rejuvenated, swarmed the streets in celebration, for it was they who had been redeemed.

As for Jack Johnson, the person who delivered this redemption to them, (if indeed it was such), he grew in legend to become what he had always been in fact: a champion among champions, and, more importantly, a man among men - and he was a good one at that.

BIBLIOGRAPHY

I. Articles

"California's Conversion." *The Independent* LXVIII (23 June 1910) p.p. 1364-1365.

Carr, F.C. "Fighting Father Time." *Colliers* VL (11 June 1920), p.p. 19, 32.

Davenport, H. "Modern Cave Man." *Colliers* VL (11 June 1910), p. 19.

Farr, Finis. "Jeff, It's Up to You!" *American Heritage Magazine* (February, 1964), p.p. 64-77.

Fyfe, Hamilton H. "What the Prize-Fight Taught Me." *The Outlook* (13 August 1920), p.p. 827-830.

Gilmore, Al-Tony. "Towards an Understanding of the Jack Johnson Confessions. *Negro History Bulletin* XXV (May 1973), p.p. 107-108.

"Johnson Wins the Great Fight." *Harper's Weekly* LIV (9 July 1910), p.p. 7-8.

Lardner, John. "The Passing of the White Hopes." Negro Digest (October, 1949), p.p. 20-31.

_____. "The Jack Johnson Era of Boxing." *Negro Digest* (November, 1949), p.p. 24-37.

Lyon, Harris Merton. "In Reno Riotous." *Hampton Magazine* XXV (September, 1910), p.p. 386-396.

"The Making of the Match." *Harper's Weekly* L111 (20 November 1909), p. 30.

Moss, Edward B. "In the Ring for a Million." *Harper's Weekly* LIV (14 May 1910), p.p. 13-14.

"No Prize Fight in California." *The Independent* LXVIII (23 June 1910), p.p. 1364-1365.

"The Psychic Collapse of Jeffries." *Current* XLIX (August 1910) p.p. 128-130.

"The Psychology of the Prize Fight." *Current Literature* XLIX (July, 1910), p.p. 57-58.

Roosevelt, Theodore. "The Recent Prize Fight." *Outlook* XCV (July, 1910), p.p. 550-551.

Ruhl, Arthur. "The Fight in the Desert." *Colliers* XLV (23 July 1910), p.p. 12-22.

Strong, Samuel M. "Negro-White Relations as Reflected in Social Types." *American Journal of Sociology* LXII (1946), p.p. 23-30.

Wiggins, William H. "Jack Johnson as Bad Nigger." *Black Scholar* (January, 1971), p.p. 34-46.

II. Newspapers and Periodicals

Boston Globe.
Chicago Broad Ax.
Chicago Daily News.
Chicago Daily Tribune.
Cleveland Gazette.
Indianapolis Freeman.
Kansas City Star.
Los Angeles Times.
New York Herald.
New York Times.
Omaha Daily News.
Omaha World Herald.
Pittsburgh Courier.
San Francisco Examiner.

III. Books

Andre, Sam and Nathaniel Fleischer. *A Pictorial History of Boxing.* Seacaucus, New Jersey: Castle Books, 1975.

Batchelor, Denzil. *Jack Johnson and His Times.* London: Phoenix Sports Books, 1956.

Chalk, Ocania. *Pioneers of Black Sport.* New York: Dodd, Mead and Company, 1975.

Cooper, Henry. *The Heavyweight Champions.* Seacaucus, New Jersey: Chartwell Books Inc., 1978.

Delaney, Martin Robinson. *The Condition, Elevation, Emigration and Destiny of the Colored People of the United States.* New York: Arno Press and the New York Times, 1968.

DuBois, W.E.B. *Souls of the Black Folk.* New York: New American Library, 1969.

Durant, John. *The Heavyweight Champions.* New York: Hastings House Publishers, 1976.

Farr, Finis. *Black Champion: The Life and Times of Jack Johnson.* New York: Charles Scribner's Sons, 1964.

Fleischer, Nathanial. *Black Dynamite: Story of the Negro in Boxing.* New York: The Ring Book Shops, 1938.

_____. *The Heavyweight Championship: An Informal History of Heavyweight Boxing from 1719 to the Present Day.* New York: G.P. Putnam's Sons, 1961.

Fredrickson, George M. *The Black Image in the White Mind: The Debate on Afro-American Character and Destiny 1817-1914.* New York: Harper and Row Publishers, 1971.

Fulks, Bryan. *Black Struggle: A History of the Negro in America.* New York, New York: Delacorte Press, 1969.

Gilmore, Al-Tony. *Bad Nigger! The National Impact of Jack Johnson.* Port Washington, New York: Kennikat Press, 1975.

Gossett, Thomas. *Race: The History of an Idea.* Dallas: Southern Methodist University Press, 1963.

Houston, Graham. *Superfists.* New York, New York: Bounty Books, 1975.

Johnson, Jack. *Jack Johnson Is a Dandy: An Autobiography.* New York: Chelsea House Publishers, 1969.

Jordan, Winthrop D. *The White Man's Burden: Historical Origins of Racism in the United States.* London: Oxford University Press, 1974.

Knowles, Louis L. and Kenneth Prewitt, eds. *Institutional Racism in America.* Englewood, New Jersey: Prentice Hall, Inc., 1969.

Lardner, John. *White Hopes and Other Tigers.* Philadelphia: J.P. Lippincott, 1951.

McCallum, John D. *The Encyclopedia of World Boxing Champions.* Radnor, Pennsylvania: Chilton Book Company, 1975.

National Association for the Advancement of Colored People. *Thirty Years of Lynchings in the United States,* 1889-1918. New York: Arno Press and the New York Times, 1969.

Rainbolt, Richard. *Boxing's Heavyweight Champions.* Minneapolis: Lerner Publications Company, 1981.

Roberts, Randy. *Poppa Jack: Jack Johnson and the Era of White Hopes.* New York: The Free Press, 1983.

Stanton, William. *The Leopard's Spots: Scientific Attitudes Toward Race in America, 1815-1859.* Chicago: The University of Chicago Press, 1960.

Sugar, Bert, et al. *100 Years of Boxing.* New York City: The Rutledge Press, 1982.

Williams, George W. *History of the Negro Race in America 1619-1880.* New York: Arno Press and the New York Times, 1968.

About the Author

Author, lecturer, teacher, Sal Fradella received his B.S. degree in history and secondary education at Dominican College of Blauvelt, New York and his M.A. in history from Western Connecticut State University. He now resides in Millbrook, New York with his wife Cheryl and son Peter.

Information about forthcoming books in this series, videos and personal appearances by the author can be obtained through the Branden Publishing Company.